Honored to have
met you!
love,
Marion

(443) 722 7955

DEDICATION

Dedicated to my David, my best friend, late husband, and soul mate of almost 30 years. He died in an accident overseas while serving in the military a month before coming home to retire. We met and fell in love during my first few months at Bible College.

David had already been there two years and I am so thankful God saved him for me. He chose me to love and marry. We married before the school year was over and he graduated from Bible College. We then ventured off to a branch ministry and he finished his undergraduate degree and served in ROTC. While at Bible College, we heard Pastor Richard Wurmbrand, the co-founder of Voice of the Martyrs. Pastor Wurmbrand was in prison for 14 years. Seven of those years were solitary confinement. This was because he would not stop sharing the Gospel with prisoners during the communist rule in Romania. David and I were so moved by his testimony and felt called to help protect freedoms in our country; specifically, to preserve the freedom of religion.

David loved his 4 children on earth, Christian, Grace, Noah, and Faith; and now he is with our babies Mercy and Moses in Heaven.

He loved our church community and the Body of Christ and a huge servant's heart. David often stopped and helped people who had broken down on the side of the road and would never take money. And a kabillion other acts of love and service to the world around him.

He often told me I was his soul mate and best friend. I had love unconditional from him for almost 3 decades.

Grief unbearable came the evening I received the death notification from two soldiers who knocked on the door. My daughters were home hearing it right alongside with me. I had just finished doing a Bible devotional time with my one daughter on "though I walk through the valley of the shadow of death..." a few minutes

before the knock. The Holy Spirit was preparing us... As I was being told, I remember hearing the Holy Spirit ask "Do you trust me? Can I use you?" My pain was so great beyond even being able to breathe, but I did not want it to be in vain. I did not want it to be lost and not used for a greater good and purpose. Yes God, yes GOD, I trust YOU; use me.

David, you were such a Gift from God to me and I am forever grateful and blessed you were my husband and I look forward to the Greatest Reunion ever...Heaven!

Many of these prayers are inspired from the grief, pain, and loss of my beloved David.

ACKNOWLEDGEMENTS

I would like to thank my son Noah for the beautiful picture he painted for me some years ago that hangs in my family room over my fireplace. The picture became the inspiration for the book cover. The red in it reminds me of the grief God bore when Jesus bled and died for us. The low-key yellow sun reminds me of the sunset of someone passing and at other times the sunrise of new things God does in our lives every day. Thank you for such a painting that speaks to me, son. I hope and pray the book cover touches your soul too.

Noah has such a gift for capturing through paintings and photographing amazing moments and perspectives so you may see more of his work in the future.

My friend Ella wrote a poem about her mom passing and she graciously allowed me to use it later in the book.

Thank you, Ian, for continuing to work with me and helping me grow in the computer and technology world. It is so easy for my mortal flesh to get stuck and give up or not even want to learn new things in this area. I am thankful God brought a kind and patient young man to help and work well together.

Thank you to my daughter Grace for continuing to work as my editor. I am appreciative for her input and suggestions and her gift in this area touches me. Sometimes I override her because I want it to be my voice at times even if it is not grammatically correct. My bad, not hers.

And finally, GOD, I am so thankful for how much YOU have walked through the valley of the shadow of death first and how YOU are there with me when I must pass through them at times. How do people do this without YOU GOD!? I am forever grateful I do not have to do life without YOU. Maybe GOD, someone who reads this prayer book will meet YOU special for the first time and have this tremendous help of YOU. I pray many who know YOU God will grow closer to YOU. Every day we need YOU God, especially in our times of grieving. Only YOU have the true comfort, help, and grace to carry us through. Sometimes I say it's hard enough with GOD, but impossible without HIM. It is not because of YOU God; it is because of the broken world we are in and our own fallen nature. With YOU we can make it. We can go forward one heartbeat at a time, one breath at a time, one footstep at a time... and over time YOU spread the waves of grief further apart, so we do not drown.

TABLE OF CONTENTS

QUIRKS

Some of the quirks you may see in this prayer book...sometimes I think I must wait for perfection to finish the product...but I have decided to no longer wait for that and I'm sure I will learn some things and do it a bit differently in the future.

*I capitalize all of GOD... early Jewish writing would leave out vowels in honoring GOD, believing He cannot be contained in a word. I have chosen to make GOD all caps as a way of saying I honor YOU as I speak these words to YOU. I also use pronouns for GOD with capital letters ...How can I ever just say "he" or "you" when He is the "HE" and the "YOU" is not just any you. YOU are not small in my eyes but the biggest and best and I'm trying to convey that in some way to others. Help me and all who read these prayers be reminded each time we see YOU and YOUR we are literally talking to GOD!!!

*Maybe someday I will have an official editor, but I didn't want someone to try to sway me from my vision. Also, trying to coordinate with another person was too much currently. It was one more thing holding me back from completing this book that I decided to let go.

*I used large fonts to make it easier to see in the morning before even your first cup of coffee (lol) and for the visually impaired. I appreciate it as I get older - hope some others do too!

*I also use different fonts because I like the change ups and not seeing the same for hundreds of pages. I appreciate seeing the new sections of the book they represent.

*Writing something that leads us closer to GOD has been on my heart since 1989. I finished writing the prayers in 2016. It seems there have been more challenges and obstacles along the way than I could have imagined finishing the journey of a book. It's been at the top of the bucket list to "git er done" these last couple of years especially after I had Covid in 2021.

*It has also been my heart's desire to leave a legacy to my children, grandchildren and any future generations to know and seek God.

When you see imperfections, please "grace grace"!

HOW TO USE THIS PRAYER BOOK!

*Make it personal - say what you want to say if you aren't feeling the morning prayer.

*Feel free to write comments or your words in the margins...make it your own.

*Some days will be very significant for you. For example, on Jan 5, that is the Anniversary of my husband going Home to Heaven, so my prayer is "I'm broken". If the prayer of the day doesn't fit or you don't like it, that's ok, just pass over it and say or write your own little prayer.

When it's a special day of yours and you want to say or write in your own prayer, go ahead, and write the year down. Years later, you have a prayer book diary to remember and look back on.

*I encourage you to write the year on each day you say the prayer. You can look back and think "Wow, I prayed this prayer on this day 2022 with YOU, Lord!" or "I prayed this prayer on this day the last 3 years". As time passes, prayers may have different value and meanings. Prayer with GOD grows, changes, and fluctuates because it is a Relationship! (Capital "R" intentional)

*Sometimes I write a key word or phrase down to remember something that happened that day. For instance, the day I flew to Iraq to volunteer with Samaritan's Purse, I wrote "flying to Iraq today to work with Samaritan's Purse 2017" next to the prayer that day.

The next year on that day, I can thank GOD for the safe flight and amazing time with caring for the wounded and dying, along with the prayer of that day.

*If you want to keep praying and talking to GOD, please do!

*This prayer book is a help, not an end all. That's what the "..." is for. You can keep on going, the little prayers help you get started. They are prayer starters...not short microwave prayers.

*As you use this prayer time, you will find yourself thinking up more and more of your own prayers and your own voice in praying to GOD...that's awesome...go with it. Prayer time with GOD is personal.

*Get ready to hear GOD throughout your day after prayer starters...! GOD speaks and keeps on speaking and the best way to hear Him is to hear the Word of GOD and read it. He is a GentleMan waiting for you. Invite Him in with your prayer.

INTRODUCTION

"Lord, I hope this prayer book brings many closer to YOU in prayer times."

I humbly confess I'm not a subject matter expert in prayer or grief. I wrote it because I have a passion to bring others into a desire to spend time with our God in all areas of our life through prayer.

I write this book from a personal journey regarding grief and my walk with GOD in it. The hope from my heart is maybe some will find help in their grief and a closer walk with Jesus in their prayer life.

Sometimes because of culture, religious beliefs, and personal thoughts, we think we must suppress our thoughts and feelings in times of grief from GOD. He already knows everything we think and feel. When we feel safe going to Him about anything, we are comforted that GOD hears, GOD listens, and we are more open to hearing GOD throughout the day.

We have opened our hearts to Him to let His Spirit, His Words, and His comfort flow.

He can use others to comfort you. He might use sunsets or hearts in unusual places. He uses worship songs that release a flow of tears and then comfort. He uses messages from the pulpit. He uses His Word, the Bible. All along, He is kind and patient and doesn't force us. He is gentle during our grief and suffering.

He can even use this little prayer each day...helping you to see others have spoken or cried your prayer. The prayer invites GOD in to make a difference. He is the Comforter. He will comfort, love, and hold you in your spirit. Trust that He knows how you feel and knows as the perfect loving Abba (Daddy God) how to help heal His child's grief. Trust Him!

ABOUT THIS BOOK

This book will not undo your grief or even necessarily relieve it, but it can help you be honest with your thoughts, feelings, wishes and wants in the midst of your grief with GOD. He is the only One Who can truly comfort your deepest grief. Praying or crying out these little prayer starters invites Him into your grief to hear and help you.

If all you do is read through these little prayers each day, it will not be enough. With all my heart I encourage you to find a great church to hear GOD, read His Word, and seek fellowship with other believers. If you have not received the Gift of Salvation and Eternal Life, please see that section towards the end of the book. The greatest comfort in time of loss is GOD. For those who love Him, He is working all things together for good.

At the beginning of each month, I have written some Grief thoughts to help you...I have spread it out over the year because often we can only receive little bits of help and information at a time as the grief can crowd out hearing, learning, listening etc.

17

If any prayer makes you feel worse or is too much to pray, pass over it. Maybe it will help you think of your own words you want to cry out to GOD and that is perfect. Go with that. On the days it's a heavy prayer ask GOD to minister to you during the day and coming days. He knows there are burdens on the grieving and broken hearted and He wants to lift them and heal us.

Any daily prayer starter can continue. If it doesn't, you have still opened the door to GOD to come in and minister to your soul and spirit and often to your body and mind too.

These prayers can be heavy and hard to read. A prayer is a heart's cry to God and allowing God to minister back to you throughout the day. If it's a prayer you don't want to pray, you can say your own prayer that day. I am just trying to give you prayers to release thoughts you may be holding inside of you. It is so much healthier for your body, soul, and spirit to give them to God.

THE BEST PART OF THE BOOK!!!

THE VERY BEST PART OF THIS BOOK IS NOT THE PRAYERS YOU PRAY BUT LISTENING BACK FOR GOD ALL DAY LONG BECAUSE YOU OPENED THE DOOR TO YOUR SOUL TO HIM WITH YOUR PRAYER!

THE STILL SMALL VOICE STILL SPEAKS! READING THE BIBLE, HEARING MESSAGES FROM YOUR PASTOR, AND BIBLE STUDIES HELP YOU HEAR GOD'S WORDS. HIS WORDS ALIGN WITH HIS TRUTH IN THE BIBLE AND ALWAYS ARE ACCOMPANIED WITH HIS LAVISH GRACE AND MERCY. AFTER PRAYING, WAIT ON GOD...LISTEN FOR HIS STILL SMALL VOICE IN YOUR SOUL AND SPIRIT!

BECAUSE OF HIS GRACE,

Maid Marian

P.S. I CALL MYSELF MAID MARIAN BE-
CAUSE I AM HONORED TO BE A HAND
MAIDEN OF THE LORD! YET HE CALLS
ME FRIEND! CAN YOU BELIEVE OUR
CREATOR CALLS US TO BE HIS
FRIEND? WOW! YAY GOD AND THANK
YOU!!

I HOPE YOU LET HIM BE YOUR
FRIEND...THERE IS NOT GREATER!

JANUARY GRIEF THOUGHTS
WHAT DO WE GRIEVE?

There are many things we grieve.
Often, we think of it in terms of
losing a parent, spouse, child, or
sibling. We can add grandparents,
grandchildren, cousins, aunts, un-
cles, nieces, nephews ...Then there
are friends, close friends, best
friends, and on and on...

We also grieve many other things!
You are free to grieve whatever you
need to grieve. None of the areas
listed are in any order and you
may think of things you grieve
that are not mentioned here.

21

We grieve...

The passing of parents

The passing of spouses

The passing of child/children

The passing of siblings

The passing of grandparents

The passing of grandchildren

The passing of aunts/uncles

The passing of cousins

The passing of nieces/nephews

The passing of best friends/friends

The passing of our Pastor and spiritual mentors

The passing of people we work with

The passing of people in our neighborhood

Death by suicide

Death by addiction

Death by Homicide

A miscarriage

A stillbirth

The death of a dream

The death of a vision

The death of a marriage/divorce

The loss of never marrying

The loss of never knowing parent(s)

The loss of never bearing a child

The loss of not being able to have
more children

The grief of not being allowed to
see a loved one, child or adult

The loss of never having a sibling or
same sibling

A prodigal child

An addicted family member or loved one

The loss of a job

The loss of a Home

The loss of all your possessions

The grief of injustice

The grief of seeing no hope

Loss of youth and getting closer to the end

Grief from trauma and abuse

Grief from rejection and hatred

Grief from an accident

Grief from wounds, scars, and loss of body parts

Grief from Injuries

Grief from diseases

Grief from Disabilities

Grief of our own sin

The grief of our regrets, coulda, shoulda, wouldas

The grief of others sin

And most of all we grieve GOD with our sin!

My point is there are many things that bring grief, and it is a personal journey for each of us!

No wonder we need help with grief! Maybe there is something you grieve, and it is not on this list, but GOD knows. He sees, He cares...bring it to HIM. He is the One Who can make a difference...everything else is temporary and like a Band-Aid on the biggest hurt you have. Lay your grief at His Feet and let Him comfort, love, and help you.

We were not created for grief. God is there to carry us and help us go forward in life despite our loss and grief. It's your choice...I pray you let Him!

If you do not see something you have grieved, fill in the blank with your word or thought_____

_____

Keep writing if you need to!

January 1

It's me GOD,

Where do I start?...

January 2

It's me GOD,

Let this not be in vain...

January 3

It's me GOD,

Though I walk through the valley
of the shadow of death...

January 4

It's me GOD,

It hurts so bad...

January 5

It's me GOD,

My heart is breaking...

January 6

It's me GOD,

I can't believe YOU bottle me
tears...

January 7

It's me GOD,

I grieve GOD...

January 8

It's me GOD,

It feels so dark...

January 9

It's me GOD,

I don't know what I'm doing...

January 10

It's me GOD,

I miss doing life with someone...

January 11

It's me GOD,

I'm drowning...

January 12

It's me GOD,

I can't stand the pain...

January 13

It's me GOD,

Carry me...

January 14

It's me GOD,

I hate change...

January 15

It's me GOD,

Your flowers people sent are beautiful...

January 16

It's me GOD,

Help me face today...

January 17

It's me God,

Sometimes I feel I will never really be happy again...

January 18

It's me GOD,

Comfort me...

January 19

It's me GOD,

Hear my cry...

January 20

It's me GOD,

I can't breathe...

January 21

It's me GOD,

I am still alive...

January 22

It's me GOD,

So much to be afraid of...

January 23

It's me GOD,

Sometimes it really hurts...

January 24

It's me GOD,

I love hearing YOU...

January 25

It's me GOD,

Please restore what I have lost...

January 26

It's me GOD,

I need rest for my soul...

January 27

It's me GOD,

Your burden is light, but it feels so heavy right now...

January 28

It's me GOD,

I can't do life alone...

January 29

It's me GOD,

I can't believe this is happening...

January 30

It's me GOD,

Sometimes I'm paralyzed with inde-
cision...

January 31

It's me GOD,

I'm running to YOU...

FEBRUARY GRIEF THOUGHTS

WAVES OF GRIEF

During some of my nursing career, I worked in hospice for about 8 years. I believed it to be a privilege to walk with patients and family down that sacred path. I stopped working there once I lost my beloved David as I knew it would be too emotional for me to be in that setting. I learned a great lesson from GOD during that time, and I would often comfort those I cared for with this beautiful picture GOD gave me. He showed me early on in grief, it is like waves constantly hitting us and feeling like we will drown living in this pain, suffering and loss. Over time, He spreads the waves of grief apart or we would drown. When waves of grief hit, they can feel as intense as those first waves of grief... but go through it... and they will pass. An important things is if we get "stuck" in our grief we need to seek help.

The first year after suffering severe loss and grief all the "firsts" are especially difficult.

I found the second year to be harder than I thought it would be. I thought it should feel easier since all the "firsts" were done, but in some ways, it was harder because the reality of the loss sets in more. That made life seem harder at times.

Some in the Jewish culture acknowledge 1000 days of loss and mourning. This is around 3 years. I found personally in the third year of loss some of the frequent grief and mourning had started to spread further and further apart. Love never ends and because of it the grief never ends, but God, in His deep love and care for us, spreads the grief waves further apart. Some days it hits us all over...but swim through the wave ...Love does not end so some grief comes even over many years...because of love.

Unresolved guilt and unforgiveness can cause grief to linger longer and deeper and are areas to seek help with. We are not made to carry these burdens.

February 1

It's me GOD,

I need a kiss from YOU today,,,

February 2

It's me GOD,

I'm so tired...

February 3

It's me GOD,

I want to hear from YOU...

February 4

It's me GOD,

Where are YOU?...

February 5

It's me GOD,

Be gentle when we wrestle...

February 6

It's me GOD,

My heart is breaking...

February 7

It's me GOD,

It's too hard...

February 8

It's me GOD,

Am I enough?...

February 13

It's me GOD,

Sometimes the memories come back
like a flood...

February 14

It's me GOD,

Be my Valentine...

February 15

It's me GOD,

I'm a mess...

February 16

It's me GOD,

Every day I need YOU...

February 17

It's me GOD,

I can't wait to open today's Gift from YOU even though I hurt...

February 18

It's me GOD,

Love was worth the sorrow...

February 19

It's me GOD,

I'm falling...

February 20

It's me GOD,

Rough day GOD...

February 21

It's me GOD,

I hate death...

February 22

It's me GOD,

I don't know what to do next...

February 23

It's me GOD,

I need to drink from Your Living
Water...

February 24

It's me GOD,

I need courage...

February 25

It's me GOD,

The coulda, shoulda, wouldas are tormenting me...

February 26

It's me God,

I feel crushed...

February 27

It's me God,

I'm bringing it all to YOU...

February 28

It's me GOD,

I cannot bear it...

February 29

It's me GOD,

I believe YOU...

MARCH GRIEF THOUGHTS

<u>*WHY IS THERE GRIEF?*</u>

Why do we grieve? We grieve because we lost something that was
important to us. In the book of
Genesis (first book of the Bible),
Adam and Eve made a choice to
trust satan more than they trusted
God and chose sin. That sin led to
the death of many things, though
not all seen at that moment. Their
bodies didn't instantly die, but over
time they did. They lost respect
and love for each other and
quickly started blaming one another for their own sin. They no
longer saw the beauty of their

bodies but felt shame and naked-
ness. One son murdered his brother.
The greatest of all losses was their
intimacy with GOD, walking in the
garden fellowshipping with Him.
Oh, sin brings such loss and grief.

In Revelation (last book of the Bible), GOD says He wipes away all
tears and all disappointments. All
these painful things we have
grieved will no longer be memories
forever for those who have received
the Gift of Salvation. Jesus gives
eternal life through His death, bur-
ial, and resurrection.

When we experience death, disease,
or divorce come, some of the most
anguishing things we grieve, they

can overwhelm us it's because we were not created for it. At times it can almost seem unbearable. We were not designed for such losses and without GOD's love and grace it can overtake us.

Woven through this book, I have shared how GOD makes the greatest difference in our grief. When we read the Bible, we see GOD is acquainted with grief. He grieves and He comforts. I pray you let Him comfort you. Fall into His Everlasting Arms, which are always there to catch you, hold you, and comfort you.

March 1

It's me GOD,

I want to feel Your presence...

March 2

It's me GOD,

So much to do, so little time...

March 3

It's me GOD,

I can't take anymore...

March 4

It's me GOD,

Whisper words of grace to me...

March 5

It's me GOD,

I tried...

March 6

It's me GOD,

I need YOUR ray of sunshine to warm my soul...

March 7

It's me GOD,

I'm not ready for this...

March 8

It's me GOD,

Flood me with YOUR presence...

March 9

It's me GOD,

Help me with the paperwork, I'm drowning in it...

March 10

It's me God,

I need others...

March 11

It's me God,

YOU never leave me...

March 12

It's me GOD,

My life feels so crazy...

March 13

It's me God,

I don't want to waste today...

March 14

It's me GOD,

I have nothing left...

March 15

It's me GOD,

I need hope, GOD...

March 16

It's me GOD,

I can't let go...

March 17

It's me GOD,

Help me to suffer well...

March 18

It's me GOD,

Keep my heart tender...

March 19

It's me GOD,

Hold me...

March 20

It's me GOD,

I don't know if I can go on...my
next steps need power from YOU...

March 21

It's me GOD,

I need godly gutz...

March 22

It's me GOD,

Chase away the darkness...

March 23

It's me GOD,

Teach me to number my days...

March 24

It's me GOD,

I don't know what to do...

March 25

It's me GOD,

Help me get it done...

March 26

It's me GOD,

Please change things GOD...YOU are
the Change Maker...

March 27

It's me GOD,

I am more than a Conqueror...

March 28

It's me GOD,

I'm broken...

March 29

It's me GOD,

I cry out to YOU! and YOU hear my cry and make a difference...

March 30

It's me GOD,

I'm beat...

March 31

It's me GOD,

I need answers...

APRIL GRIEF THOUGHTS

TEARS & WATER

TEARS...oh how many tears have you cried? Ever since I was a young girl, I have been a cry-baby. Kids would make fun of me for it, but I'm a very sensitive person and it is part of my divine design. Back then I did not know this, and I would try to open my eyes really big so the tears wouldn't drop out. Or I would try not to blink so the next blink couldn't push out the

tears or I would try to blink,
blink, blink to force the tears
to go in instead of out. Nothing
worked...it's who I am but I did
learn some wonderful things
about tears in the *Bible!*

Do you know GOD could collect
anything in the world...stars,
mountains, galaxies etc., but He
chooses to collect our tears
(Psalm 56:8)? I see this as a
tender loving picture of GOD.
Just like a Momma would gently and carefully wipe a child's
tears from their face comfort-
ing as she does, I see GOD as the
gently loving Holy Spirit wiping

my tears. I am not alone. I never was even in all those early years when I did not know this about Him.

You need lots of water to re-place the tears you shed and for the inner tears no one sees you shedding. Every cell in your body needs water, and the en-emy of your soul does not want you to drink water. Don't wait until you are thirsty or have a headache (a sign you are dehy-drated). Everywhere you go in the early months of grieving, have a bottle of water with you and drink it, don't just carry it around. When you drink it, tell yourself you are drinking "life". If you are grieving a loved one, know they would want you to be well or get well. Be intentional and take steps - one of them is drinking water! Another is to move and serve others...that will be covered in one of the later months. Drinking water is a healthy habit that can follow you for the rest of your life.

April 1

It's me GOD,

I'm stumbling...

April 2

It's me GOD,

I just want to run away...

April 3

It's me GOD,

YOU can restore what's lost...

April 4

It's me GOD

Help me put my big girl pants on...

April 5

It's me GOD,

I need YOU special today...

April 6

It's me GOD,

I feel like I will never make it...

April 7

It's me GOD,

I want to my last laps of life to be strong...

April 8

It's me GOD,

I need patience...

April 9

It's me GOD,

Some days are so long...

April 10

It's me GOD,

Let all things lead me to YOU...

April 11

It's me GOD,

Life is hard...

April 12

It's me GOD,

Help me to trust YOU...

April 13

It's me GOD,

It's so hard...

April 14

It's me GOD,

Sometimes I long to come Home...

April 15

It's me GOD,

It hurts so bad I can't move...

April 16

It's me GOD,

I need help...

April 17

It's me GOD,

Hug me God...

April 18

It's me GOD,

Help me not grow weary...

April 19

It's me GOD,

YOUR bouquets of flowers bless me...

April 20

It's me GOD,

I am such a failure...

April 21

It's me GOD,

I have so much to do...

April 22

It's me GOD,

Help me be still...

April 23

It's me GOD,

I can't stand the hurt...

April 24

It's me GOD,

Do YOU care?...

April 25

It's me GOD,

Take care of me...

April 26

It's me GOD,

Cut down the tree of anger...let
Your kindness grow in me...

April 27

It's me GOD,

I can't believe I said that...

April 28

It's me GOD,

Sometimes I'm afraid to finish...

April 29

It's me GOD,

I wish I knew how many days I had
left...

April 30

It's me GOD,

YOU are the Author and Finisher of
me!...

MAY GRIEF THOUGHTS

WRITING AND JOURNALING

Years ago, a sweet friend of
mine in church taught me
some Russian for my Teaching
English as a Second Language
certification (TESOL). We had
to learn some common
phrases of a new language so
we could better identify with
the challenges of those learning English. I chose Russian
because there were many Rus-
sians in our Baltimore Church

and Sinai Hospital ER I worked in as an RN.

My friend Ella was so kind and patient in teaching me some common phrases. I had it on a tape cassette and every day my *kids would listen to me practice my phrases as we drove to their school.*

This past year, Ella lost her mom at 88 years old. She wrote a beautiful poem, and I asked her if I could share it here in my Grief Prayerbook. I am so thankful for her beautiful words capturing some of my heart thoughts having lost my mom of 90 years old 6 months before her mom passed.

I pray this poem touches your heart and soul too.

Ella's Poem

I've always loved you more
Than I could ever say!
Now, mourn you and adore,
Since you have gone away.

You'd been my faithful friend
And refuge, all my life;
The road went and bent,
You helped me rise and thrive!

You were my lullaby,
My beacon in the night;
I've always could rely
On you, and not lose fight.

How could you leave so soon?
You've always been so strong!
I love you to the moon
And back, what did go wrong?!

The questions punch the sky,
The matrix of belief,
Bombarding with the "why?!"
Not giving sweet relief...

I grieve your sudden death,
It made me pale and numb...
You left my heart a mess,
Please, rest in peace, my mom!
By Ella Yanushevskaya

Writing and journaling can help us release some of our hurts and feelings. That is part of how this prayer book I have written came to be.

I encourage you to jot some thoughts down in this prayer book with the date. In later times, you can come back and see how GOD is moving and working on your behalf to help with your grief, beloved soul.

May 1

It's me GOD,

I ache...

May 2

It's me GOD,

I can't do it...

May 3

It's me GOD,

I feel vulnerable...

May 4

It's me GOD,

I'm in the valley, but so are YOU!...

May 5

It's me GOD,

There's not enough time in the day...

May 6

It's me GOD,

I thirst...

May 7

It's me GOD,

Let me be quick to hear YOU...

May 8

It's me GOD,

This too shall pass...

May 9

It's me GOD,

Prepare me for what's ahead...

May 10

It's me GOD,

I need strength...

May 11

It's me GOD,

Every minute I need YOU...

May 12

It's me GOD,

I am so limited...

May 13

It's me GOD,

Lead me through the darkness...

May 14

It's me GOD,

I can't believe YOUR love doesn't
depend on my heart towards YOU...

May 15

It's me GOD,

I know memories are supposed to
comfort but sometimes they really
make me hurt...

May 16

It's me GOD,

Can't keep up...

May 17

It's me GOD,

I set my heart on YOU...

May 18

It's me GOD,

Help me see YOU...

May 19

It's me GOD,

Heal me please...

May 20

It's me GOD,

Keep my heart tender...

May 21

It's me GOD,

Take it from me...

May 22

It's me GOD,

How can this be happening?...

May 23

It's me GOD,

I hurt...

May 24

It's me GOD,

Be gentle God...

May 25

It's me GOD,

Don't forget me...

May 26

It's me GOD,

I can do all things...

May 27

It's me GOD

Draw me closer...it's such a safe
place...

May 28

It's me GOD,

Can I stay in bed today?...

May 29

It's me GOD,

I fall so short...

May 30

It's me GOD,

Keep me on Your path...

May 31

It's me GOD,

Come...

JUNE GRIEF THOUGHTS

SOME OF MY GRIEF JOURNEY

I'm sharing some of my journey and the things I do to help others who are grieving. I do not write this book as a subject matter expert on grief. Some of the grief I have suffered came from losing my husband to an accident overseas as a soldier in 2009. He made it through 3 combat tours and was just about a month away from coming home to retire after almost 23 years of active duty. It was a devastating shock to me. I was so looking forward to our family time making up for all the missed birthdays, anniversaries, holidays, and kids' landmarks etc. We made so many sacrifices as a military family. My kids growing up over the years with their dad away for multiple deployments, TDYs and field exercises. We thought we would finally have David home to start making up for all the lost time he was away. It was a devastating shock to me and our four children.

My dad passed in 2012. He was how I first knew there was a God who unconditionally loved me. When I was a little girl I would wet the bed. Mom had 5 children in 6 years. She wasn't as patient as dad was in those times. I would look up at him and knew it something more than my dad, so patient and kind in those moments. Later, as I learned about God's unconditonal love, I

realized that's what he was loving
me with.

Mom passed in Christmas Eve 2021.
I grew up with 4 brothers and no
sisters so mom was my best friend.
I dedicated my first prayer book I
wrote "GOOD MORNING GOD, IT'S
ME!" to her. We were prayer warri-
ors together for many years. She
had such purpose in her elderly
years praying for all her kids and
grandkids. She use to say I am
lifting up the one who needs it the
most to God but don't tell me who
it is with a smile.

I lost 2 babies during pregnancy in
1982 and 1998. I named them
Mercy and Moses.

So many times my heart has ached to know them...but someday in Heaven I will.

As an older adult, I connected with my half-sister I only knew in my later adult years. All my life I had wished for sister love and has been a huge hole in my life. She lived on the other side of the country, so we only had a few times to meet before she died in 2010 from cancer.

I had found deep love again in 2015-16 and became engaged. I didn't think it possible and was devastated once again with the loss of a future together due to his re-occurring struggles with addictions.

I said goodbye to our two beloved dogs Shadow and Meshack after 14 and 16 years. I didn't realize how hard it was to even lose beloved pets.

I grieved two of my children's marriages ending in divorce. It was like losing children I loved and the grief for my children's heart break.

I grieve the coulda, shoulda, wouldas, with regret mixed in. I have grieved when my children or I make choices that grieve GOD and many other things listed in the January grief list.

I know so many have grieved so much more. To each of us our grief is personal, not better, or worse. I grieve easily and often. It's part of my makeup and personality, but by GOD'S grace He takes me through it, and I move forward and often experience joy and laughter be-caused of GOD! As I grieve, I cry out to HIM with little prayers and open the door for Him to come in and help heal my hurt.

Someday, I have the grandest reun-ion in Heaven with my loved ones who loved God. I think God may even have our Beloved pets too!

June 1

It's me GOD,

Hold me ...

June 2

It's me GOD,

Thank YOU for the blessing me, I had an amazing husband...

(fill in the name of someone special that went Home to Heaven that you are thankful for
_____)

June 3

It's me GOD,

Whisper words of Love to me...

June 4

It's me GOD,

Redeem and restore me...

June 5

It's me GOD,

Do YOU hear my prayers?...

June 6

It's me GOD,

I need YOU, GOD...

June 7

It's me GOD,

Move me towards YOU...

June 8

It's me GOD,

I need YOU to lighten the load...

June 9

It's me GOD,

I'm afraid...

June 10

It's me GOD,

Instruct me...

June 11

It's me GOD,

Wow, bad things happen to good
people...

June 12

It's me GOD,

I don't take it lightly YOU hear
me...

June 13

It's me GOD,

I feel like giving up, GOD...

June 14

It's me GOD,

YOU bring me hope...

June 15

It's me GOD,

Everything ends but YOU...

June 16

It's me GOD,

Help me to not drop out...

June 17

It's me GOD,

Take me away...

June 18

It's me GOD,

Your grace is sufficient...

June 19

It's me GOD,

I didn't sleep at all...

June 20

It's me GOD,

Cut down the tree of bitterness...

June 21

It's me GOD,

Hold my hand...

June 22

It's me GOD,

I'm angry...YOUR grace will help me even in anger to sin not...

June 23

It's me God,

I can't try anymore...

June 24

It's me GOD,

I can't believe YOU know the worst
about me and love me the most...

June 25

It's me GOD,

When I'm wrong help me to know
it...

June 26

It's me GOD,

I can't do it anymore

June 27

It's me GOD,

Keep me in Your way...

June 28

It's me GOD,

YOU are bigger...Thank YOU no god
comes close to YOU!...

June 29

It's me GOD,

Your love is stronger than my fear...

June 30

It's me GOD,

Help...

July Grief Thoughts

<u>GRATITUDE</u>

Grieving can really pull us under the wave. Sometimes it helps if we can count some of our blessings and things to be thankful for to rise above the grief. Maybe you are thinking you don't have much to be thankful for but if you are reading this, you have eyes, breath, a heartbeat and so much more. When you look for even the smallest things to be grateful for, your list of things snowballs. Do you enjoy seeing the sunrise or sunsets GOD paints every day? Does something tickle you and make you laugh or giggle? These are just a few of the things you can add to your gratitude list.

I bet if someone asked you to think of 1000 things to be thankful for over the days and weeks ahead and told you they would give you $1000 dollars for it, every day you would find small, medium, and big things to be grateful for. It is a mindset, and in healing and rising above the waves of grief, a heart of gratitude is like a life preserver. As I have said before it is human to grieve but we can get stuck. We need to keep moving forward so we don't get stuck in the wave. Being thankful helps us move forward from the grief. If you are grieving over a lost one, wouldn't they want you to find safe healthy ways to move forward? Being grateful is a profound tool and medicine for healing.

July 1

It's me GOD,

Sometimes it's too much...

July 2

It's me GOD,

It's so hard suffering silently...

July 3

It's me GOD,

I'm seeking YOU...

July 4

It's me GOD,

Protect me...

July 5

It's me GOD,

Revive me...

July 6

It's me GOD,

I hope I'm always pointing to YOU...

July 7

It's me GOD,

I need YOU now...

July 8

It's me GOD,

YOU are so good to me...

July 17

It's me GOD,

Help me to trust again...

July 18

It's me GOD,

I have blackness... but in YOU there is light though...

July 19

It's me GOD,

The road seems dark...

July 20

It's me GOD,

I have so many regrets...

July 21

It's me GOD,

What's next?...

July 22

It's me GOD,

Thank YOU for being such a

Father to me, GOD...

July 23

It's me GOD,

Help me turn my gaze to YOU ...

July 24

It's me GOD,

I feel like I can't do this anymore...

July 25

It's me GOD,

Are there dogs in Heaven?...

July 26

It's me GOD,

What do YOU want of me?...

July 27

It's me GOD,

Refresh my hopes...

July 28

It's me GOD,

I grieve again...

July 29

It's me GOD,

Cut down the tree of hate...let
Your tree of Love grow, grow,
grow...

July 30

It's me GOD,

So much can go wrong it scares
me...

July 31

It's me GOD,

I know YOU are there, but I wish
someone with flesh and blood
would love me again like my David did (my late husband) ...

AUGUST GRIEF THOUGHTS

MOVEMENT IS MEDICINE

Movement helps us get unstuck in
grief waves. Sometimes we need to
put our big girl or big boy pants on
many days even if we don't feel like
it and move. One step at a
time...keep moving.

Celebrate the victories of pushing
through no matter how small. I
would write down things I got done,
a load of dishes, trash out etc. One
day all I could write down was I
picked up a rubber band from the
floor, but I did something! I wrote
it down because it was a victory

over doing nothing that day, and it helps build momentum.

One of the little things I do is challenge myself with a 5-minute pick up even on the blue or very sad days. I would set a timer and see how much I could get done in 5 min, "just get 5 minutes in, Marian"! Afterwards, I would often have the motivation to keep going for another 5 or 10 minutes. It often got me going when I felt no energy to do anything. I still play this little challenge with myself to get me going when I just don't feel like doing anything. I have never done a 5- or 10-minute challenge and afterwards regretted it. This has helped me over and over and over.

I taught myself to hoola hoop from YouTube during my second year of grieving over the loss of my beloved husband. I could not hoola hoop as a child, but I always wanted to be able to do it. The first day after watching a YouTube video, I tried 10 times and gave up. I said a little prayer to God and said tomorrow I will have more time and will try 100 times. On try number 62, I got it! Now I know even when the hoop drops, it's a squat or lunge to pick it up, so it's all good. It's movement and exercise; and usually some giggles and laughter too, especially if I am with others.

The point is move, breathe, and get out of the bed or chair most days. It's ok to take a day occasionally to be sad or blue, but you can't live there...it will kill your soul and spirit and eventually your body.

August 1

It's me GOD,

I wish I could see YOU now...

August 2

It's me GOD,

Flood me with Your peace...

August 3

It's me GOD,

Pray for me, GOD...

August 4

It's me GOD,

I'm overwhelmed with life...

August 5

It's me GOD,

I'm such a procrastinator and grief makes it so much worse...

August 6

It's me GOD,

Rough night...

August 7

It's me GOD,

Life is too much for me sometimes...

August 8

It's me GOD,

Some days are so hard...

August 9

It's me GOD,

I'm hurt by what YOU allow to happen...

August 10

It's me GOD,

Be my friend...

August 11

It's me GOD,

Be gentle Lord...

August 12

It's me GOD,

All good gifts come from YOU...

August 13

It's me GOD,

I took so much for granted...

August 14

It's me GOD,

Be my friend...

August 15

It's me GOD,

My faith seems far away...

August 16

It's me GOD,

Fill me...

August 17

It's me GOD,

I'm exhausted...

August 18

It's me GOD,

I feel like I can't try any longer...

August 19

It's me GOD,

I can't stop crying...

I never thought this would happen to me...

August 20

It's me GOD,

The coulda, shoulda, wouldas tor-
ment me...

August 21

It's me GOD,

This world is crazy...only YOU
make sense and redemption out
of crazy...

August 22

It's me GOD,

I'm beat up, GOD...

August 23

It's me GOD,

It's not well with my soul...

August 24

It's me GOD,

Why did this happen?...

August 25

It's me GOD,

Why does it hurt so badly when a dog (pet) dies? ...

August 26

It's me GOD,

I am weak...

August 27

It's me GOD,

I need a fresh Word from YOU,
GOD...

August 28

It's me GOD,

Why do things have to die? ...

August 29

It's me GOD,

I am weary...

August 30

It's me GOD,

I trust YOU...

August 31

It's me GOD,

I'm tired...

SERVING AND HELPING OTHERS

Sometimes, thinking about serving others may seem like too much for your grieving soul, but God often uses things we think won't help or we can't do. It may even seem counterintuitive to you. But somewhere wrapped up in the mysteries of God and His ways, there is a blessing, distraction, and a sense of joy in helping others even when we still have our own hurt and pain.

I am not recommending running from our grief work and healing,

but I have seen so many times
how "helping others" can help our
own hurt and pain.

Sometimes, there is a sense of
"Wow, it could be worse and I'm
so glad it's not". Sometimes, serving others is a distraction and
relief from our own grief. Sometimes, it's seeing we live in a world
bigger than our own hurts and
sorrow and that we have something we can give to sometimes,
it's the joy and peace we feel afterwards of the good works and
deeds we have done with God's
grace to do so. Sometimes, it's the
hope of tomorrow that I have
something to offer it because of

what I did today, even when I
thought I was too bankrupt.

September 1

It's me GOD,

Thank YOU I will not taste death
like an unbeliever...

September 2

It's me GOD,

I sorrow...

September 3

It's me GOD,

Show me the way...

September 4

It's me GOD,

Be my shield...

September 5

It's me GOD,

I need help to navigate the waters of life...

September 6

It's me GOD,

I am missing my man...
(fill in who or what you are missing_____)

September 7

It's me GOD,

My life is crazy...

September 8

It's me GOD,

Your burden feels very heavy to-day... thank YOU, YOU pick it up and carry it or I couldn't move...

September 9

It's me GOD,

Jesus, Jesus, Jesus...

September 10

It's me GOD,

I need an increased filling from YOU...

September 15

It's me GOD,

My tank is feels empty...

September 16

It's me GOD,

Cut down the tree of fear...

September 17

It's me GOD,

Refresh my soul...

September 18

It's me GOD,

I can't move...

September 19

It's me GOD,

The valley is dark...

September 20

It's me GOD,

Sometimes I don't understand Your
ways...

September 21

It's me GOD,

Thank YOU I can come as I am...

September 22

It's me GOD,

Do I have to get up? ...

September 23

It's me GOD,

I'm sorry I haven't been talking to YOU...

September 24

It's me GOD,

I suffer silently, it is so hard to do that...

September 25

It's me GOD,

Sometimes I can't wait to see them...

September 26

It's me GOD,

I can't take it anymore, help...

September 27

It's me GOD,

Your trees are breathtaking balm
to my soul...

September 28

It's me GOD,

Every hour I need YOU...

September 29

It's me GOD,

So much pressure, GOD...

September 30

It's me GOD,

I'm having trouble believing...

Your faith will hold me though...

OCTOBER GRIEF THOUGHTS

GRIEFSHARE

I found GriefShare to be one of the most helpful things that spoke to my grief.

"Grief Share is a network of thousands of grief recovery support groups meeting around the world. Griefshare is a program with direction and purpose. With Griefshare, you will learn how to walk the journey of grief and be supported on the way. It is a place where hurting people find healing and hope."

"Your GriefShare group is designed to help you recover from the deep hurt of loss. Your GriefShare experience includes three key elements that work together to guide your healing process. We encourage you to commit to taking part in all three aspects of GriefShare"

GriefShare groups usually meet for 13 weeks, and the time includes a video, a support group, and a work book."

I participated in 3 different groups over time, because I was unable to go every week. The information was so helpful I wanted to hear and participate in each of the weeks.

The videos were of some well-known people and also ordinary people like you and me. I liked the variety of experiences shared.

The workbook was very thorough and included so much. Here are the chapter/session headings:

Session 1: Living with Grief

Session 2: The Journey of Grief

Session 3: The Effects of Grief

Session 4: When Your Spouse Dies

Session 5: Your Family and Grief

Session 6: Why?

Sometimes in grief, we can only process a little at a time. My encouragement is a little is better than none. I hope you will step out in faith and find a GriefShare group when you feel ready. If you loved someone very, very much and their grief was deep or hindering their ability to go forward; what would you tell them? Would you want them to get the help they need? GriefShare is another layer of helping in the grief work and healing process.

GriefShare's phone: 800 395-5755

International: 919 562-2112

www.griefshare.org

If you are depressed and have any suicidal thoughts or plans, please get professional help!

This world will not be better off without you!

Talk to someone who will listen and can help you and get professional mental health help!!

National suicide/crisis hot line is 988

October 1

It's me GOD,

I'm in trouble...

October 2

It's me GOD,

Please redeem things...

October 3

It's me GOD,

There is none like YOU...

October 4

It's me GOD,

I need fresh manna...

October 5

It's me GOD,

I am lonely...

October 6

It's me GOD,

Be the center of my life...

October 7

It's me GOD,

Let me feel Your Hand in mine...

October 8

It's me GOD,

Fill my emptiness of heart...

October 9

It's me GOD,

I hurt so badly...

October 10

It's me GOD,

There will always be a hole...

October 11

It's me GOD,

You are full of grace to me...

October 12

It's me GOD,

Help me to forgive...

October 13

It's me GOD,

I have darkness, Lord...

October 14

It's me GOD,

I don't know how I'm gonna do it...

October 15

It's me GOD,

Can I stay under my blankets today?...

October 16

It's me GOD,

Does anyone care? ...

October 17

It's me GOD,

I need to eat Your Bread of Life...

October 18

It's me GOD,

I'm afraid...

October 19

It's me GOD,

I'm trusting YOU, GOD...

October 20

It's me GOD,

YOUR peace does pass understand-
ing...

October 21

It's me GOD,

I need Your strength...

October 22

It's me GOD,

Please wipe my tears...

October 23

It's me GOD,

I didn't sleep good...

October 24

It's me GOD,

Cut down the tress of unforgiveness...

October 25

It's me GOD,

Help me to live...

October 26

It's me GOD,

I need a hug from You today...

October 27

It's me GOD,

One step forward ...two steps back-
wards...

October 28

It's me GOD,

I miss my Mom so much...

October 29

It's me GOD,

YOU help me so many times,
thank YOU...

October 30

It's me GOD,

Hear my prayer...

October 31

It's me GOD,

Sometimes I'm afraid of the dying process...

NOVEMBER GRIEF THOUGHTS

REDEMPTION

/ believe one of the biggest griefs we suffer is the death of those closest to us and at times the fear of our own dying and death. We may think or ask, "why is there death?" We may ask God "why do we have to lose loved ones? Why do we die?"

Earlier in January Grief Thoughts, I wrot about the fall of mankind in the garden and how sin caused suffering and death to come into this world and all our lives. As we live and grow in life, we have many blessings and wonderful things. We also suffer, have disappointments, hard work, rejections and at times things that seem unbearable. Over time, we see our bodies start to age and lose the abilities we once had when we were younger. Over the decades, our outward beauty fades. When I worked in hospice nursing, often as the elderly were dying, the family would have a beautiful photo on their wedding day or a military photo when they were young and strong. I would look at the picture and think they are barely recognizable.

Time captures moments but God captures Eternity and Redemption. He loves us too much to leave us in the world that is constantly breaking down along with our bodies. We do the best we can to stay healthy and take care of ourselves and our world, but it is never enough. At some point for each one of us, Mercy brings us Home to Heaven if we have accepted the Gift of Jesus as God WHO took all our sins on Him on the Cross and died and rose three days later. God allows death as a consequence for sin, but in His love, He gives life after death for those who accept the Gift of Salvation. When we breathe in our last breath in this life and body, death allows us to breathe out that breath in our new life in Heaven forever.

There is so much that can be taught on life, death, Heaven, and Eternity. All our life we can learn and grow with God. I could fill thousands of pages of what God has shown, taught and done in my life over 6 decades but it would only be someone else's story. I challenge and encourage you to seek GOD and let Him write stories in your heart and life. Let Him meet your journey of grief and redeem it. None of us can escape grief, death, or loss.

Even with God, your next steps may seem very hard, but without Him in your life, I would say it's almost impossible to recover to the place where you find great joy and hope for your next day.

November 1

It's me GOD,

Soften my heart...

November 2

It's me GOD,

Help me not give up...

November 3

It's me GOD,

Rekindle my faith...

November 4

It's me GOD,

I'm falling...catch me...

November 5

It's me GOD,

I need You to fill me...

November 6

It's me GOD,

I long for You God...

November 7

It's me GOD,

Life is a vapor...

November 8

It's me GOD,

Doing life hurts...

November 9

It's me GOD,

Help me do the difficult...

November 10

It's me GOD,

My hope is in you...

November 11

It's me GOD,

I can't go on without YOU...

November 12

It's me GOD,

Find me GOD...

November 13

It's me GOD,

Flow through me...

November 14

It's me GOD,

I feel like such a failure...

November 15

It's me GOD,

I need YOUR peace...

November 16

It's me GOD,

Life is short...got to get it done...

November 17

It's me GOD,

I can't, but YOU can...

November 18

It's me GOD,

I need to be closer...

November 19

It's me GOD,

Come Lord...

November 20

It's me GOD,

I feel far from YOU...

153

November 21

It's me GOD,

It's almost too much to bear...

November 22

It's me GOD,

I'm angry with YOU GOD...forgive me for feeling this way...

November 23

It's me GOD,

I can't do it without YOU...

November 24

It's me GOD,

I feel like I'm failing the test...

November 25

It's me GOD,

I'm trying...

November 26

It's me GOD,

I can't take it...

November 27

It's me GOD,

It is well with my soul..

November 28

It's me GOD,

I don't want to talk to anyone to-day!...

November 29

It's me GOD,

I need to rest in YOU...

November 30

It's me GOD,

I'm afraid for what's ahead...
knowing YOU are there, helps me
take the step forward...

DECEMBER GRIEF THOUGHTS

LET GOD LOVE, HOLD, AND HEAL YOU!

This life is hard enough with GOD, not because GOD is hard but because we are in a fallen world from sin. We are broken and flawed at birth, but so much potential and purpose has been placed in each of us by GOD. The things we grieve over and some so heavy we think we can't breathe or take our next breath want to paralyze, crush, or consume us. We can't go on, but with

GOD'S strength, love, and grace, we take one breath at a time and one step forward to live the life we have. It is not a perfect life nor are circumstances easy, but for those who love GOD, He will work it together for good. Nothing else in life can save or heal us in our grief but GOD... <u>please let Him!</u>

As you travel down your road of life you will start to see you can have joy, laughter ,and hope again. You will go through waves of grief over your lifetime, but GOD will spread them apart. Lay down the burdens and baggage that want to continually pull you down under.

We must use our freedom of choice and volition and let go of what hinders us and hold onto to the Eternal things that set us free.

I hope these little daily prayers of honest heart and lament to GOD help you to release them to HIM. Our grief and sorrow is too much for us

to carry through life 24/7.
Let go and let GOD love you
and carry you each day as
much as much as you need
HIM to, He never wearies!

December 1

It's me GOD,

May my fruit remain...

December 2

It's me GOD,

I need YOU...

December 3

It's me GOD,

My faith feels like it's dying...

December 4

It's me GOD,

Sometimes I feel like I just want to
close my eyes and not wake up...

December 5

It's me GOD,

I feel alone...and then I realize I'm not alone because YOU are with me

December 6

It's me GOD,

I can't stand life... it hurts too much...

December 7

It's me GOD,

Help me be still and know You are GOD...

December 8

It's me GOD,

Renew my spirit...

December 9

It's me GOD,

Show me which path to take...

December 10

It's me GOD,

Please take care of me...

December 11

It's me GOD,

Open my heart...

December 12

It's me GOD,

I need a fresh Word from YOU...

December 13

It's me GOD,

Minister to me ...I hurt...

December 14

It's me GOD,

Flood me with Your love...

December 15

It's me GOD,

I hate my life sometimes...

December 16

It's me GOD,

I can't even walk unless YOU hold my hand...

December 17

It's me GOD,

Refresh me...

December 18

It's me GOD,

I need direction...

December 19

It's me GOD,

Hear my anguish...

December 20

It's me GOD,

I can't stand life sometimes...

December 21

It's me GOD,

Don't let me drown in my sorrow...

December 22

It's me GOD,

How do people do life without
knowing You deeply? ...

December 23

It's me GOD,

I feel stuck in grief...

December 24

It's me GOD,

Today, help me begin again...

December 25

It's me GOD,

The door of hope is born today...

December 26

It's me GOD,

Come Lord quickly...

December 27

It's me GOD,

Let my tears and sorrow be a reservoir of life for others...

December 28

It's me GOD,

Please take care of me...

December 29

It's me GOD,

I hate being alone and YOU whisper back "lonely but not alone" ...

December 30

It's me GOD,

Help me to finish...

December 31

It's me GOD,

Help me to finish strong!...

SCRIPTURE VERSES

On Grief, Suffering, Loss...

GOD's heart in the Bible (The Word of GOD or Scripture or verses are other names for it) will comfort and help more than anything. It will not only unlock help, hope, and comfort, it will give you so much more then you can imagine.

I am writing some verse references and a key word about the scripture. Different versions of the Bible can seem easier or more understandable.

Look for a Bible version you can understand.

OLD TESTAMENT

Genesis 28:15   I am with you

Joshua 1:9   discouraged

Nehemiah 8:10   joy of Lord strength

Job 3:26   no peace

Psalm 9:9   Lord is refuge

Psalm 23:4   comfort

Psalm 25:16-17   lonely and afflicted

Psalm 27:4-5   Lord will keep me

Psalm 6:6   pillow soaked with tears

Psalm 30:5 weeping night joy morning

Psalm 34:18   close to brokenhearted

Psalm 46:10   be still

Psalm 48:1   guide even unto death

Psalm 49:15   redeem, take me to HIM

Psalm 55:22   cast your cares on Lord

Psalm 73:26   God is the strength

Psalm 86:17   Lord helps and comforts

Psalm 147:3   heals brokenhearted

Lamentations 3:32   compassion

Isaiah 25:8   wipe away tears

Isaiah 40   walk and not faint

Isaiah 41:10   I will strengthen you

Isaiah 43: 1-4   precious in His sight

Isaiah 57:1-2   they find rest

Hosea 13:14   ransomed from power of

grave

NEW TESTAMENT

John 16:22	I will see you again
Luke 23:43	you will be with me
Romans 8:28	those who love GOD
Romans 8:38-39	nothing separates us
Romans 14:8	whether we live or die
1 Corinthians 13	Love
1 Corinthians 15:21-22	made alive
1 Corinthians 15:42-45	resurrection
1 Corinthians 15:54-	imperishable
2 Corinthians 4: 17-1	unseen is eternal
2 Corinthians 5:8	absent from body
Romans 8:38-39	nothing separates us
1 Peter 5:7	cast your care on GOD
1 Thessaloniansn4:13-17	those who died
Revelation 21:4	tears, no more death

"IT'S ME GOD!"

SERIES CONTINUES

I am blessed that you are reading these little breath prayers and whispered prayers to GOD called *"It's Me GOD, I Grieve!*

This book is the second in a series of *"It's Me GOD!"* prayer books:

"It's Me GOD, Good Morning!

"It's Me GOD, I Grieve!"

Soon to be published:

"It's Me GOD, Help!"

"It's Me GOD, Thank-YOU!

"It's Me GOD, Good Morning! Volume 2

If this prayer book has helped you to have a little bit deeper and closer times with talking and hearing GOD, I hope you will want more in this series of *"It's Me GOD!"*. *Giving a review on Amazon helps others hear about this unique prayer book too!*

Look for them on Amazon.com

SUPPORT FOR THIS BOOK

I believe in missions and helping others. One dollar from each book sold in the "It's Me GOD, I Grieve!" series will be donated to the TAPS organization. TAPS personally assisted our family significantly after the loss of my husband and my children's dad over the past 13 years. The following is a copy of their mission statement from their website so you can see how much they do to walk beside fallen military member's families...

THE MISSION OF _TAPS_

"TAPS provides compassionate care to all those grieving the death of a military loved one.

Since 1994, TAPS has provided comfort and hope 24/7 through a national peer support network and connection to grief resources, all at no cost to surviving families and loved ones.

TAPS provides a variety of programs to sur-
vivors nationally and worldwide. Our National Military Survivor Seminar and Good
Grief Camp has been held annually in
Washington, D.C., over Memorial Day week-
end since 1994. TAPS also conducts regional survivor seminars for adults and
youth programs at location across the
country, as well as retreats and expeditions
around the world. Staff can get you connected to counseling in your community
and help navigate benefits and resources.

If you are grieving the loss of a fallen service member, or if you know someone who
can us our support the TAPS 24/7 National
Military Survivor Helpline is always availa-
ble toll-free with loving support and resources at 800-959-TAPS (8277)."

TAPS is a national nonprofit 501(c)3 Veter-
ans Service Organization and is not part
of, or endorsed by, the Department of De-
fense.

Gift of Eternal Life and SALVATION!!!

Have you met my Lord and Savior? If not, the Father, the Son Jesus, and Holy Spirit come to your heart and soul right now gently knocking giving you the choice to have a personal relationship with GOD! Jesus came to this world and lived the only perfect life and then died on a Cross to pay for our sins. When we believe He died for our sin personally, we have the Gift of Salvation imparted to us. We are born again, His child adopted into His family forever. He will never leave or forsake you.

If you believe and receive this GIFT of Salvation, I urge you to find a wonderful church where you can grow as a babe in Christ and learn so many wonderful things about GOD. As my Aunt Gemma would say, 'He is crazy about you!" Reading the Bible, GOD's Holy Word, will reveal so much to you about the One Who waits for you to talk and walk with Him. Oh, to be saved and loved unconditionally is the most amazing thing ever. So much awaits you, and I pray you will keep discovering the Truth about GOD through prayer, the Bible, church, the Body of Christ, and His beautiful world He created for you.

With grace and because of grace,

Maid Marian

P.S. May these little heart prayers from your heart to His help you start on His road of love, grace, and truth!

About the Author

Loving, praying, and talking to GOD has been a part of her life since she was a little girl. She grew up in Pittsburgh, PA
and became a Nurse. A call from the Lord moved her to Bible College in Massachusetts where she met and fell in love with her husband David. After hearing Pastor Wurmbrand from Voice of the Martyrs speak at their Bible College, they both felt led by GOD to serve in the military as their mission field and defend
America's freedom for a combined 50 plus years.

The Baltimore Maryland area has been her mission field the past 25 years. She completed her 2-year Bible College degree over a 31-year period and is on the 50-

year plan for her 4-year degree. She believes never quit learning about GOD and His Word - no matter where you go or what you do, you are never too old to grow and serve with GOD. She has been involved in short term medical missions and missionary work in Haiti, Iraq, Ghana, Togo, Korea, France, Germany, and Hungary throughout the decades.

Writing and sharing about GOD has been in her soul along with women's ministry for over 40 years. She has been published in women's ministry newsletters and devotionals and enjoys teaching women Bible studies in various settings. She also conducted workshops at regional and national seminars with PWOC and spoke at various women's ministry events over the years.

She has been blessed with a Godly husband (in Heaven since 2009), 4 children on earth (Christian, Grace, Noah, and Faith) and 2 in Heaven (Mercy & Moses with Dad) and 4 grandchildren. Even her children's names were chosen to cry out her testimony of God!

She served in the Army Nurse Reserves as part of her missionary field for 23 years, retiring as a Lieutenant Colonel. She desires to forever be active duty in the Lord's Army till she is promoted to Heaven.

She loves crafting, gardening, and painting. She enjoys staying active and learning new things such as hula hooping from YouTube in her 50s after 62 tries over 2 days. She also likes hiking, camping, and sharing flower bouquets from her yard with as many women as possible to just say "GOD loves you and is thinking of you"!

This book kicks off the second in a series of "It's Me GOD!':

"It's Me GOD, Good Morning!"
"It's Me GOD, I Grieve!"
"It's Me GOD, Help!"
"It's Me GOD, Thank YOU!"

Her greatest passion in life is to be a cheerleader for GOD; showing how wonderful He is and leading others into a more personal relationship with Him.

Her Mission Field is wherever GOD has her. She loves to laugh and smile for Jesus and her favorite cheer is "YAY GOD"!

FINAL NOTE !!!

Many of these prayers I can hardly believe I wrote in my anguish, sorrow, and grief. I don't even remember praying some of them, but I did. I could have whitewashed this book so it wouldn't show as much transparency and rawness, but I want it to show how hard and deep grief can be. It's critical to keep turning to God in it in prayer. Prayer has been a lifeline for me and from God to me for decades. I pray you listen for HIM too.

My salvation started with a prayer, my life continues with prayer and someday my prayers will be face to FACE to the ONE I pray to and listen for.

Love, Maid Marian

Yay GOD! 3 10 23 1330

Made in USA - North Chelmsford, MA
1365032_9798377454724
03.28.2023 1301